Understanding Floating Point Numbers

Concepts in Computer Systems
(Volume 2)

Eric Sakk, Ph.D.

Preface

This book is the second in a series developed for readers interested in various aspects of computer systems and computer technology. It is meant to be both concise and introductory. Some basic familiarity with binary numbers is assumed. The material presented can be used to supplement courses relevant to computer science and computer engineering anywhere from the high school level up to the college level.

Table of Contents

Chapter One: Introduction

This book is meant to be a continuation of Volume 1 which introduced a spectrum of topics related to binary integers in the context of computer systems. While this volume on floating point numbers is meant to be 'stand-alone', basic understanding of binary integers and hexadecimal representation is assumed. If the reader needs a primer on these topics, this author has no qualms about making a shameless plug for Volume 1. Floating point numbers are not more difficult to understand than integers, but the interested reader should have the requisite background in order to fully understand the finer details of the material presented here.

A floating point number is simply a convention for describing numbers with a decimal point and is specifically defined for computer system applications. For instance, when one uses a variable of type 'float' in a typical programming language, a convention and a standard must be agreed upon so that all (useful) computers can understand each other. The goal of this text then is to develop and present, in a principled way, the structure of the floating point representation. To do this, we have built a roadmap that starts out with binary integers in Volume I and now progresses, in this current volume, from binary fractional numbers to binary scientific notation and, finally, to the floating point representation.

The path from binary integers to binary scientific notation is a mathematical one. The final step from scientific notation to the floating point representation has inherent subtleties and conventions required in order for computer systems to make practical use of the representation.

Chapter Two: Unsigned Fractional Binary Numbers

Let us first relate the computer systems terminology to some equivalent mathematical terminology

The term 'unsigned fractional' number means that we are referring to a 'nonnegative rational' number.

The fractional number will necessarily include an integer part and a fractional part. For example in base 10, $(12.045)_{10}$, $(0.213)_{10}$ and $(3.14)_{10}$ are all fractional numbers each with an integer part and a fractional part.

Mathematical Note: Recall that computer systems always work with finite numbers of bits (i.e. finite 'precision'); hence, computers can only provide a truncated approximation to most numbers. Since any given number will be represented with some finite '*precision*', such an approximation (i.e. the 'terminating' decimal) must, by definition, be rational.

Unsigned Fractional Decimal Numbers

Given the discussion in the introduction, we should be quite familiar with base expansions for representing unsigned integers with 'm' digits in base 10 or 'm' bits in base 2. For example, with m=5 digits in base 10, it should be clear that

$$(31024)_{10} = 3\times10^4 + 1\times10^3 + 0\times10^2 + 2\times10^1 + 4\times10^0$$
$$= 3\times10000 + 1\times1000 + 0\times100 + 2\times10 + 4\times1$$

Or, using m=4 bits in base 2,

$$(1011)_2 = 1\times2^3 + 0\times2^2 + 1\times2^1 + 1\times2^0$$
$$= 1\times8 + 0\times4 + 1\times2 + 1\times1$$
$$= (11)_{10}$$

In order to elevate the *unsigned integer representation to include a fractional part,* we can simply look to the base 10 expansion as a guide.

Consider a 5-digit expansion allowing for two decimal places:

10^2	10^1	10^0	.	10^{-1}	10^{-2}	
x 100	x 10	x 1		x 1/10	x 1/100	
5	2	7	.	3	8	= 527.38

In addition to the ones place, the tens place and so on for nonnegative powers of 10 in the base expansion, the tenths place, hundredths place and so on must be included to the right of the so-called 'decimal point'. Notice that, in order to represent the fractional part of a number, *negative powers of the base* must be considered.

Negative Powers of 2

Anticipating the need for negative powers of two when describing unsigned fractional binary numbers, we present the following table.

n	2^n	=	=
-1	2^{-1}	1/2	0.5
-2	2^{-2}	1/4	0.25
-3	2^{-3}	1/8	0.125
-4	2^{-4}	1/16	0.0625
-5	2^{-5}	1/32	0.03125

Binary to Decimal Conversion

Evaluating fractional binary numbers requires fluency with both nonnegative and negative powers of two. Consider converting the following 6-bit binary number to decimal where 3 bits are reserved for the integer part and 3 bits are reserved for the fractional part:

2^2	2^1	2^0	.	2^{-1}	2^{-2}	2^{-3}
x 4	x 2	x 1		x 1/2	x 1/4	x 1/8
1	0	1	.	0	1	1

$$(101.011)_2 = 4 + 1 + 0.25 + 0.125 = (5.375)_{10}$$

Notice, combinatorial considerations dictate that there must be exactly $2^6 = 64$ unique 6-bit sequences. One of these sequences happens to be 101011. Only when the choice is made to use three bits for the fractional part in an unsigned expansion can we attribute meaning to those bits and conclude that

$$(101.011)_2 = (5.375)_{10} .$$

Once the '*precision*' is specified (i.e. how many bits are used for describing the fractional part), the numerical weight of each bit position becomes known and the equivalent decimal value can be determined.

Consider Table 2.1 that lists all possible 4-bit binary numbers. Additionally, in this example, we have chosen to use two of the available four bits for representing the fractional part. With this choice, it becomes possible to attribute meaning to each binary sequence and compute an equivalent decimal value.

2^1	2^0	.	$2^{-1} =$ 0.5	$2^{-2} =$ 0.25	$= (\quad)_{10}$
0	0	.	0	0	0.00
0	0	.	0	1	0.25
0	0	.	1	0	0.50
0	0	.	1	1	0.75
0	1	.	0	0	1.00
0	1	.	0	1	1.25
0	1	.	1	0	1.50
0	1	.	1	1	1.75
1	0	.	0	0	2.00
1	0	.	0	1	2.25
1	0	.	1	0	2.50
1	0	.	1	1	2.75
1	1	.	0	0	3.00
1	1	.	0	1	3.25
1	1	.	1	0	3.50
1	1	.	1	1	3.75

Table 2.1: A list of all possible 4-bit fractional numbers and their equivalent decimal values when two bits are used to represent the fractional part and two bits are used to represent the integer part

Given this prescription, numbers between 0 and 3.75 are specified to within a value of 0.25 (i.e. the weight of the least significant bit).

Multiplication and Division by 2

Given a fractional binary number, the following statements are true:

- *Multiplying a number by 2* in base 2 is equivalent to a *left shift* of the binary sequence by one bit
- *Dividing a number by 2* in base 2 is equivalent to a *right shift* of the binary sequence by one bit

Let's consider some examples to demonstrate these principles.

Example: Assuming m=7 bits with two of those bits used to represent the fractional part,

$2 \times (3.25)_{10} = 2 \times (00011.01)_2$
$= (00110.10)_2$ (left shift of 3.25 by one bit)
$= (6.5)_{10}$

$4 \times (3.25)_{10} = 2 \times (2 \times 3.25)$
$= 2 \times (00110.10)_2$
$= (01101.00)_2$ (left shift of 6.5 by one bit)
$= (13)_{10}$

To summarize,

$(3.25)_{10}$	$(00011.01)_2$
$(6.5)_{10}$	$(00110.10)_2$
$(13)_{10}$	$(01101.00)_2$

Each successive multiplication by two has shifted the binary sequence to the <u>left</u> by one bit.

Example: Assuming m=7 bits and using three of those bits for representing the fractional part,

$(12)_{10}$	$=$	$(1100.000)_2$
$(12)_{10} / 2$	$(6)_{10}$	$(0110.000)_2$
$(6)_{10} / 2$	$(3)_{10}$	$(0011.000)_2$
$(3)_{10} / 2$	$(1.5)_{10}$	$(0001.100)_2$
$(1.5)_{10} / 2$	$(0.75)_{10}$	$(0000.110)_2$
$(0.75)_{10} / 2$	$(0.375)_{10}$	$(0000.011)_2$

In this case, each successive division by two has shifted the binary sequence to the <u>right</u> by one bit.

Exercises

1. In a manner similar to Table 2.1 with m=4 bits, construct a new table assuming, instead, that 1 bit is used for representing the fractional part. What is the smallest increment between any two numbers on the list?

2. Construct a table similar to the one above with m=5 bits assuming 3 bits are used for representing the fractional part. What is the smallest increment between any two numbers on the list?

Chapter Three: Decimal to Binary Conversion

In order to exercise concepts and develop intuition regarding fractional binary numbers, we will be introducing three approaches to performing decimal to binary conversion:

- Ad hoc intuition
- Basic Algorithm
- Base Expansion Algorithm

Similar algorithms for integers were discussed in Volume 1 and only some slight (yet, computationally significant) modifications are required to deal with the fractional part. A very important theme of this chapter is to highlight _practical limitations of finite precision_ that the practitioner must be made aware of. In addition, a solid foundation will be established for upcoming chapters introducing binary scientific notation.

Ad Hoc Intuition

Ad hoc intuition requires fluency with negative powers of two in order to decompose a fractional number into sums of powers of two. Consider the table below that lists all possible 4-bit binary numbers where we have chosen to use three bits for representing the fractional part.

2^0	.	2^{-1}	2^{-2}	2^{-3}	$= (\quad)_{10}$
x 1		x 1/2	x 1/4	x 1/8	
0	.	0	0	0	0.000
0	.	0	0	1	0.125
0	.	0	1	0	0.250
0	.	0	1	1	0.375
0	.	1	0	0	0.500
0	.	1	0	1	0.625
0	.	1	1	0	0.750
0	.	1	1	1	0.875
1	.	0	0	0	1.000
1	.	0	0	1	1.125
1	.	0	1	0	1.250
1	.	0	1	1	1.375
1	.	1	0	0	1.500
1	.	1	0	1	1.625
1	.	1	1	0	1.750
1	.	1	1	1	1.875

So, in order to convert $(1.625)_{10}$ into its equivalent binary description $(1.101)_2$, one would first have to see that
$$(1.625)_{10} = 1 + 1/2 + 1/8 \rightarrow (1.101)_2$$

Notice that the smallest increment between any two numbers on the list is $(0.125)_{10}$ which is the weight of least significant bit.

It is *extremely important* to recognize that the accuracy of any decimal to binary conversion will be *limited by the finite number of bits specified for the fractional part* of the binary number. Hence, we must anticipate that

a given computation will, in most cases, be an <u>approximation </u> to some desired value,

The only case for which the conversion could be exact is where the decimal number to be converted is expressible as an exact, finite sum of powers of two. Then, if there are enough bits specified to represent the finite sum, the conversion would be exact.   In the opposite case, the binary fractional part must necessarily be a truncated version of the base 10 number and; therefore, can only be a rational approximation.

Basic Algorithm

With small numbers of bits, an ad hoc decomposition is possible; however, as the number of bits increases, it becomes sensible to have a programmable algorithm at hand in order to solve the base conversion problem.

Given an unsigned fractional number $(x)_{10}$, the algorithm presented in this section requires
1. Choosing an integer 'K' to be a power of 2 such that
$$0 \le x \le 2^K$$
   in order to specify the number of bits for the integer part.
2. Specifying how many bits 'L' are desired for the fractional part in order to be known to within an increment of 2^{-L}.

The minimum value of 'K' is easily ascertained by computing
$$K = int(\log_2(x)) + 1$$
where 'int' takes the integer part of the value.

Given the values of K and L, the following steps will generate a binary approximation to some given value $(x)_{10}$:

1. Set: b=[ ] (i.e. 'b' is an empty binary string)
2. Set: k=K-1
3. If $x < 2^k$

      b=[b, 0] (i.e. append a zero to the binary string 'b')

  Else

      b=[b, 1] (i.e. append a one to the binary string 'b')

      Set: $x = x - 2^k$
4. Set: k=k-1
5. if $k \ge -L$, then go to step 3
6. stop

This is an iterative algorithm that works by _peeling off successive powers of two_ in decreasing order and can be easily programmed with a construct such as a 'for' or 'while' loop.

Let's look at an example and walk through each iteration when x=$(3.380)_{10}$ and L=3 bits are chosen to represent the fractional part. Observe,

$$K = int(\log_2(3.380)) + 1 = 2$$

Hence, we will choose 'K' to be the minimum number of bits required to represent the integer part and 'L' bits will be used for the fractional part for a total of

$$m = K + L = 5 \text{ bits}$$

to approximate x=$(3.380)_{10}$.

Iteration k=K-1=1:
    a. $3.380 \geq 2^1$ → b=[b, 1] = 1
    b. Set: $x = x - 2^k = 3.380 - 2^1 = 1.380$
    c. Set: k = k-1 = 0

Iteration k=0:
    a. $1.380 \geq 2^0$ → b=[b, 1] = 11
    b. Set: $x = x - 2^k = 1.380 - 2^0 = 0.380$
    c. Set: k = k-1 = -1

Iteration k=-1:
    a. $0.380 < 2^{-1}$ → b=[b, 0] = 110
    b. Set: k = k-1 = -2

Iteration k=-2:
    a. $0.380 \geq 2^{-2}$ → b=[b, 1] = 1101
    b. Set: $x = x - 2^k = 0.380 - 2^{-2} = 0.130$
    c. Set: k = k-1 = -3

Iteration k=-3:
    a. $0.130 \geq 2^{-3}$ → b=[b, 1] = 11011
    b. Set: $x = x - 2^k = 0.130 - 2^{-3} = 0.005$
    c. Set: k = k-1 = -4
'stop' since k<-L.

The above algorithm yields the approximate result that
$$(3.380)_{10} \approx (11.011)_2$$

Since $(11.011)_2 = (3.375)_{10}$, this approximation is accurate to within a value of
$$(3.380\text{-}3.375)_{10} = (0.005)_{10} < 2^{-7}.$$

This indicates that the next binary value of one would be encountered in the 2^{-8} position of the fractional part

$$(3.380)_{10} \approx (11.01100001)_2$$

which most likely would be considered acceptable if only L=3 bits of fractional precision were specified. Of course, other choices of 'x' need not lead to a small approximation error; the precision depends upon by the value specified by 'L'.

Base Expansion Algorithm

Consider a base 10 number $(y)_{10}$ such that
$$0 \leq y < 1$$
which clearly must be of the form $y = 0.d_1d_2d_3 \ldots$ where the digit in the ones place is assumed to be zero.

Given our understanding of binary numbers, the algorithm introduced in this section can be phrased conceptually as follows:

1. Output the value in the ones place of 'y'
2. Form a new value by multiplying the fractional part of 'y' by 2 (i.e. left shift the number by one bit)
3. Call this new value 'y'
4. Go to step 1 until all bits are output.

Step 1 inspects the ones place which we recall, for integers, is equivalent to computing a number '**mod 2**' (see, for example, Volume 1 of this series). Step 2 keeps the number bounded between zero and one and then left shifts that number by one bit. Step 4 indicates that the algorithm will iteratively inspect the ones place after each left shift takes place.

Mathematical Aside: Consider a more formal phrasing of the above steps. Given the initial condition '$y_0 = y$', perform the following iteration for $k = 0,1,2,3,4, \ldots$.

$$y_{k+1} = \begin{cases} 2y_k & \text{if } 0.0 \leq y_k \leq 0.5 \\ 2y_k - 1 & \text{if } 0.5 < y_k < 1.0 \\ 0 & \text{if } y_k = 1.0 \end{cases}$$

It turns out that this description falls into a class of so-called 'piecewise linear' iterative mappings and shift mappings which have been demonstrated to have a rich set of properties including chaotic and fractal behaviors. Here we must remain focused on the topic of finite decimal to binary conversions.

Based upon the steps outlined above, the following pseudocode implements the above algorithm designed to extract each bit from the fractional part of a number.

Given some number 'y' where $0 \leq y < 1$ and 'L' is the number of desired fractional bits.

1. Set: m=L
2. Output: the ones place of y
3. Set: y=2 x (fractional part of y)
4. Set: m=m-1
5. If m ≥ 0, then go to step 2
6. stop

The output binary number will then be of the form
$$0.b_1b_2b_3 \dots b_L \quad .$$

Let's look at an example and walk through each iteration when $y=(0.5625)_{10}$ and L=5

Iteration m=5:
    a. y=0.5625 ➜ Output: 0
    b. Set: y = 2 x 0.5625 = 1.125
    c. Set: m = 5 - 1 = 4

Iteration m=4:
    a. y=1.125 ➜ Output: 1
    b. Set: y = 2 x 0.125 = 0.250
    c. Set: m = 4 - 1 = 3

Iteration m=3:
    a. y=0.250 ➜ Output: 0
    b. Set: y = 2 x 0.250 = 0.50
    c. Set: m = 3 - 1 = 2

Iteration m=2:
    a. y=0.50 ➜ Output: 0
    b. Set: y = 2 x 0.50 = 1.0
    c. Set: m = 2 - 1 = 1

Iteration m=1:
    a. y=1.0 ➜ Output: 1
    b. Set: $y = 2 \times 0.0 = 0.0$
    c. Set: $m = 1 - 1 = 0$

Iteration m=0:
    a. y=0.0 ➜ Output: 0
    b. Set: $y = 2 \times 0.0 = 0$
    c. Set: $m = 0 - 1 = -1$
'stop' since m<0.

The resulting output sequence is ordered from MSB first to LSB last; hence, we obtain the desired result that $(0.5625)_{10}$ = $(0.10010)_2$.

The above algorithm is designed to extract the fractional part of a number; however, it is easily modified in order to extract the integer part. Isolating the integer part (as was presented in Volume 1) requires iterating a series of _right shifts (i.e. divide by 2)_ in order to inspect the ones place.

Summary

Hopefully at this point, some fluency with fractional numbers has been imparted to the reader. In addition, numerical subtleties attributable to finite precision have also been addressed. More underlying subtleties of finite precision such as rounding errors will be explored in the exercises. The work put into understanding these early chapters will prove indispensable for grasping the material in upcoming chapters dealing with binary scientific notation and floating point representations.

Exercises:

1. Test other input values of x and L in the basic algorithm to understand and internalize how this algorithm is working. Make sure you address issues of accuracy in light of the finite precision given your choice of L.

2. Test other input values of y and L in the base expansion algorithm to understand and internalize how this algorithm is working. Make sure you address issues of accuracy in light of the finite precision given your choice of L.

3. Consider converting $y=(0.6875)_{10}=(0.1011)_2$ with only L=2 bits reserved for the fractional part. In this case, both the basic and base expansion algorithm would yield $(0.10)_2=(0.5)_{10}$; however, the sum of the remaining powers of two indicate that the closest approximation should be $(0.75)_{10}=(0.11)_2$. Hence, in the form presented, neither algorithm attempts to '**round up**' based upon the value of the next binary digit associated with the next lower power of 2. Try to modify these approaches by adding some steps that will inspect the next lower power of 2 and round the number accordingly.

Chapter Four: Scientific Notation

The next step along our path to understanding floating point representations is to translate our understanding of binary fractional numbers into scientific notation.

Decimal Scientific Notation

As usual, we rely on our basic understanding of base 10 in order to make the leap. Let's consider some examples in order to review some terminology and make some observations that can be readily extrapolated to base 2.

$$(+28.30513)_{10}$$
$$= +0.02830513 \times 10^3$$
$$= +0.2830513 \times 10^2$$
$$= +2.830513 \times 10^1$$
$$= +28.30513 \times 10^0$$
$$= +283.0513 \times 10^{-1}$$
$$= +2830.513 \times 10^{-2}$$
$$= +28305.13 \times 10^{-3}$$

$$(-5.7302)_{10}$$
$$= -0.057302 \times 10^2$$
$$= -0.57302 \times 10^1$$
$$= -5.7302 \times 10^0$$
$$= -57.302 \times 10^{-1}$$
$$= -573.02 \times 10^{-2}$$

Scientific notation describes a number using three parts: the **sign**, the **significand** and the **exponent**. For example, considering
$$+283.0513 \times 10^{-1}$$
in the above example implies that
Sign = +
Significand = 283.0513
Exponent = -1.

Assuming base 10, the sign, the significand and the exponent are enough to uniquely describe a fractional number.

Recall that multiplication by the base value results in a left shift by one digit and division by the base value results in a right shift. The above examples illustrate this principal when the base value is 10. Left shifts and right shifts of numerical sequences give the impression that the decimal point of the significand is being 'moved' (if one is in the reference frame of the decimal point, then the digits appear to be shifted; and, if one is in the reference frame of a given digit, then the decimal point appears to be moving). Hence, multiplying by 10 (i.e. a left shift) results in 'moving' the decimal point to the right by one digit, and dividing by 10 (i.e. a right shift) is equivalent to moving the decimal point to the left by one digit.

Observation:
- When a left (right) shift takes place in the significand by one digit, in order to maintain equality, the corresponding exponent must be decreased (increased) by one

Binary Scientific Notation

Given the above terminology and observations for base 10, we should expect nothing different when the base value is changed to 2.

$(+10.011)_2$
$$= +0.10011 \times 2^2$$
$$= +1.0011 \times 2^1$$
$$= +10.011 \times 2^0$$
$$= +100.11 \times 2^{-1}$$
$$= +1001.1 \times 2^{-2}$$

$(-1010.01101)_2$
$$= -10.1001101 \times 2^2$$
$$= -101.001101 \times 2^1$$
$$= -1010.01101 \times 2^0$$
$$= -10100.1101 \times 2^{-1}$$

Again, the sign, significand and the exponent are enough to uniquely specify a number. Considering the value

$$-10.1001101 \times 2^2$$

we may conclude the following:

Sign = -
Significand = -10.1001101
Exponent = +2.

Left shifts by one bit still imply that the decimal point is moved to the right and, in base 2, indicate a multiplication 2. Right shifts by one bit still imply the decimal point is moved to the left and, in base 2, indicate division by 2. Therefore, assuming base 2, the following is still true:

Observation:
- When a left (right) shift takes place in the significand by one bit, in order to maintain equality, the corresponding exponent must be decreased (increased) by one

Normalized Form

Given the above examples, it should be clear that many choices exist for representing a number in scientific notation. We therefore invoke a convention that will turn out to be sensible from a computer systems perspective.

The <u>normalized form</u> of a number has its first nonzero bit (or, digit) in the ones place.

The concept is quite straightforward. Let's look at some examples of normalized numbers.

<u>Base 10</u>
$$(-5.7302)_{10} = -5.7302 \times 10^0$$

<u>Base 2</u>
$$(+10.011)_2 = +1.0011 \times 2^1$$

If a number is not observed to be in normalized form, it is a simple exercise to make the conversion by shifting the significand and adjusting the exponent. For instance, the binary number

$$-10101.101 \times 2^3$$

Is not normalized. To convert to normalized form, the significand can be adjusted by shifting the sequence four bits to the right requiring the exponent to be increased by four

$$-1.0101101 \times 2^7$$

or, expressed in terms of our three components
Sign = -
Significand = 1.0101101
Exponent = +7.

Storage Convention

Given the above terminology and concepts, we can begin to suggest a general framework for how a computer might represent and store a fractional number in scientific notation:

Sign	Exponent	Significand

Sign
Since the sign can be either positive or negative, only one bit is required
> Sign Bit = 0 if positive
> Sign Bit = 1 if negative

Exponent
Since the exponent can be either negative or nonnegative, we need to specify its binary representation. Because of its pervasiveness, one might select the signed two's complement representation as a candidate. However, for reasons that will become clear later, we will introduce the so-called '**excess**' representation in the next chapter.

Significand
We choose to represent the significand in **normalized form** implying that that the ones place will necessarily contain a one.

The foundation and concepts for defining floating point representation have, in principal, been established. Since the sign bit is well-defined by a single bit, we must solidify in greater detail how the significand and the exponent will be represented. The next set of chapters present the finer points regarding the structure outlined above.

Chapter Five: Excess Representation

We must address how the exponent associated with the binary scientific notation of a number will be represented. In digital systems there are many possible choices for representing signed integers. For instance, the signed two's complement representation is the standard for signed integer data types on most computer systems. The only constraint comes from the number of bits specified. Combinatorial considerations always dictate that, given 'm' bits, there are exactly 2^m unique binary sequences that can be constructed. Any efficient representation should devote about half of the set of available binary sequences to negative exponents and the remaining portion to positive and zero exponents. For floating point numbers, we will choose to introduce the excess representation. As we begin to unfold the floating point description, it will become obvious why this is a sensible choice. For now, we begin by defining and describing the representation.

Excess n

In the '*excess n*' representation
- $n=(2^{m-1}-1)$ where 'm' is the number of bits used to represent the exponent.
- The most negative number is $-n$
- The most positive number is $+2^{m-1}$

Examples

n	m bits	Most negative value	Most positive value
3	3	-3	+4
7	4	-7	+8
15	5	-15	+16

Already we can notice subtle differences between excess n representation and the two's complement representation for signed integers when it comes to characterizing the most negative and most positive values.

Converting Decimal to Excess n

Given a value x in base 10 such that

$$-n \le (x)_{10} \le 2^{m-1}$$
$$\text{where } n = (2^{m-1} - 1),$$

the following steps are used to <u>generate an m-bit excess n signed binary integer</u>:
1. **Form the sum: z = x+n (i.e. add n to the decimal number)**
2. **Convert z to an unsigned binary integer**

<u>Examples</u>

Excess 15 → m=5
Let $x = (5)_{10}$
   1. $z = 15 + 5 = 20$
   2. $(20)_{10} = (10100)_2$ unsigned
Conclude:
     $(5)_{10} = (10100)_2$ (Excess 15)

Converting Excess n to Decimal
The inverse process back to excess n is quite straightforward simply 'undo' the steps listed above:
1. Convert unsigned binary to decimal
2. Subtract n

Excess 15
Given $y = (00011)_2$
   1. $(00011)_2 = (3)_{10}$ (unsigned)
   2. $3 - 15 = -12$
Conclude:
     $(00011)_2 = (-12)_{10}$ (Excess 15)
You can double check by performing the conversion of $(-12)_{10}$ back to excess n.

Important Observations

To see the bigger picture, let's construct a table in order to illustrate some more general observations.

Excess 3

$(.)_{10}$	Add 3	Convert to unsigned
+4	7	111
+3	6	110
+2	5	101
+1	4	100
0	3	011
-1	2	010
-2	1	001
-3	0	000

Notice that half the list is devoted to positive integers and the other half is devoted to non-positive integers.

The Sign Bit
The leftmost bit of excess n representation indicates the sign of the exponent:
- 1 → positive
- 0 → not positive

So, without needing to know the actual value, we may conclude, for example, that
$$(1011\ 1110\ 0110)\ \text{excess 2047}$$
is a positive number.

Easily recognizable sequences

n	m bits	$(\ .\ )_{10}$	Excess n
3	3	+4	111
		+1	100
		0	011
		-1	010
		-3	000
7	4	+8	1111
		+1	1000
		0	0111
		-1	0110
		-7	0000
15	5	+16	11111
		+1	10000
		0	01111
		-1	01110
		-15	00000

It is a straightforward exercise to draw the following general conclusions given the excess n representation

- The most negative number is a string of 'm' zeros
- $(-1)_{10}$ converts to a sequence beginning with a zero followed by a string of ones and ending with a zero.
- $(0)_{10}$ converts to a sequence beginning (from left to right) with a zero followed by a string of ones.
- $(+1)_{10}$ converts to a sequence beginning (from left to right) with a one followed by a string of zeros.
- The most positive number is a string of 'm' ones

So, without performing any calculations, given m=8 bits (and, hence, $n=2^7-1=127$), the following excess 127 values are immediately recognized:

$(+128)_{10}$ = (1111 1111) excess 127
$(+1)_{10}$ = (1000 0000) excess 127
$(0)_{10}$ = (0111 1111) excess 127
$(-1)_{10}$ = (0111 1110) excess 127
$(-127)_{10}$ = (0000 0000) excess 127

Exercises

1. Construct a table that relates decimal values to their excess n representation for n=15. Make sure you highlight easily recognizable sequences in order to verify the properties listed in the text.

2. Compare and contrast the signed two complement representation with the excess n representation.

Chapter Six: Floating Point Representation

Given the foundation from the previous chapters for fractional numbers, scientific notation and the excess representation, we are now in a position to begin defining the floating point representation. For the purposes of illustration, we will use an 8-bit example to explain how the bits are to be allocated and arranged for the significand, the exponent and the sign bit. After we have worked through all the fine details in this chapter and the next, we will then provide examples containing larger numbers of bits (for example, as in the IEEE floating point standard).

Two major features of the floating point representation are as follows:
- The **_significand_** is represented in **_normalized form_**.
- **_The Hidden Bit_**:
  Since, in <u>normalized form</u>, the first bit preceding the decimal point is <u>always equal to one</u>, it will not be explicitly stored in the bit representation of the significand. <u>This bit will be 'hidden'</u>. Note the bit is not being 'removed', this would change the value of the significand. Instead, it is assumed to be implicitly part of the number and is only represented when it becomes necessary to perform a calculation or output a result. This approach to representing the floating point number will provide us with <u>one more bit of precision in the significand</u>.

Consider the following 8-bit example demonstrating the floating point representation:

Sign bit = 1 bit
Exponent = 3 bits (➔ excess 3)
Significand = 4 bits

Sign (1 bit)	Exponent (3 bits)	Significand (4 bits)

Given this choice, we need to develop a sense for the maximum and minimum values that can be represented. In addition, we must also make the reader aware of issues concerning numerical accuracy given the bit precision (i.e. the number of bits) chosen for the significand.

Bit Precision and Numerical Accuracy

Let's consider representing the decimal value $(.725)_{10}$. A decimal to binary conversion can be computed to produce the repeating binary sequence

$$(.725)_{10} = (0.\ 10111\ 0011\ 0011\ 0011\ \ldots)_2$$

Recall that a numerical sequence generated by a rational number can only be a 'terminating' decimal or a 'repeating' decimal. In base 10, $(.725)_{10}$ (= 725/1000) is a 'terminating decimal' and, in base 2, a periodic, 'repeating' sequence is generated. Only when the number can be decomposed into a finite sum of powers of two will the base 2 sequence terminate. Both terminating sequences requiring more bits than provided by the significand and repeating sequences must necessarily be truncated given the finite bit precision. Under such circumstances, we can expect that the floating point representation will, at best, end up as an approximation to the numerical values.

Converting the above value to _scientific notation in normalized form_ and assuming 4 bits for the significand (with the implied 'hidden bit' to the left of the decimal point):

$$(.725)_{10} \approx +1.0111 \times 2^{-1}$$

Sign Bit = 0 (since positive)
Exponent = 010 (in excess 3)
Significand = 0111

The floating point 8-bit representation then becomes

0	010	0111

or simply

0010 0111

Let's investigate the accuracy of this approximation by converting it back to decimal. To do this, we must restore the hidden bit

$$+1.0111 \times 2^{-1} = (0.10111)_2$$
$$= 1/2 + 1/8 + 1/16 + 1/32$$
$$= (0.71875)_{10}$$

This yields a difference of
$$(.72500 - 0.71875) = 0.00625.$$

The numerical precision is defined by the number of bits specified in the representation:

The precision of a floating point number is determined by the number of bits allocated for the significand.

The bit precision will clearly have an effect on the numerical accuracy of the approximation when a binary sequence in truncated. We will explore this issue more deeply in the next chapter.

Maximum and Minimum Values

The maximum and minimum values (i.e. those having the largest magnitude) are generated by the largest possible significand and the largest possible exponent. For our example using the largest possible 4-bit significand and the largest possible 3-bit exponent in excess 3, we obtain

$$1\ 111\ 1111 = -1.1111 \times 2^4 = -31.0$$
$$0\ 111\ 1111 = +1.1111 \times 2^4 = +31.0$$

As for the binary integer case, practical computational considerations dictate that we pay close attention to values that define boundaries within the representation. For the floating point case, the next chapter will address several such cases.

Exercises:

a. Assuming the 8-bit floating point representation discussed in this chapter, determine the floating point representation for the following values:

    a. $(0.151)_{10}$
    b. $(0.75)_{10}$
    c. $(0.49218750)_{10}$

Make sure you convert your result back to the original in order to observe any limitations on accuracy given the precision.

Chapter Seven: Practical Considerations for Numerical Implementation

Based upon the specification of the sign bit, the exponent and the significand, the floating point representation is defined for almost any numerical value. In this chapter we address special cases that must be considered in order to ensure computational continuity and numerical completeness of the description.

Representing Zero

In the floating point representation, zero cannot be normalized. For this special case, we invoke the following **_definition for zero:_**

i. Exponent = -n (excess n) (i.e. the most negative possible exponent = string of zeros)
ii. Significand = 0 (i.e. a string of zeros)

Observe that the sign bit can be either one or zero implying that, computationally, there can be a +0.0 and a -0.0. For the 8-bit example, zero would look like

-0.0 ≡

1	000	0000

+0.0 ≡

0	000	0000

<u>Pay close attention</u>. Based upon the representation, the values having the smallest magnitude would have been those with the smallest significand and the most negative exponent:

$$-1.0000 \times 2^{-3} = -0.1250 = 1\ 000\ 0000$$
$$+1.0000 \times 2^{-3} = +0.1250 = 0\ 000\ 0000.$$

However, we are now reserving these binary sequences to *define a value of zero*. **This, in turn, implies that**

$$\textbf{-1.0001} \times \textbf{2}^{\textbf{-3}} = \textbf{-0.1328125} = \textbf{1 000 0001}$$
$$\textbf{+1.0001} \times \textbf{2}^{\textbf{-3}} = \textbf{+0.1328125} = \textbf{0 000 0001}$$

now become the smallest normalized values that can be represented.

Underflow and Overflow

<u>Underflow</u> occurs when a computation generates a value between
    a. +0.0 and the smallest positive value
    b. -0.0 and the smallest negative value

For instance, continuing our 8-bit example, calculations such as
$$0.2 \times 0.2 = +0.04$$
$$-0.1 \times 0.1 = -0.01$$
would both result in an underflow since,

$$\textbf{+0.0} < +0.04 < \textbf{+0.1328125}$$

and

$$\textbf{-0.1328125} < -0.01 < \textbf{-0.0}.$$

Alternatively, **<u>overflow</u>** occurs when the result of a calculation ventures *outside* the most positive or most negative boundary. In our representation example,

$$1\ 111\ 1111 = -1.1111 \times 2^4 \quad = -31.0$$
$$0\ 111\ 1111 = +1.1111 \times 2^4 \quad = +31.0$$

This definition is similar to the signed integer case and we need to pay close attention to calculations that can lead to the overflow condition. For example,

$$+31.0 + 2.0 = +33 .0$$
$$-31.0 - 3.0 = -34.0$$
$$10.0 \times 7.2 = 72.0$$

are all examples of calculations that extend outside the boundaries of the representation given the specified number of bits for the sign bit, the significand and the exponent.

The following diagram illustrates the overflow and underflow regions for our 8-bit example.

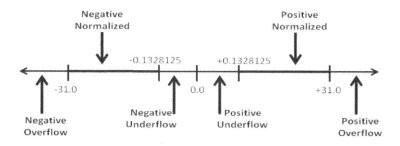

Representing the Underflow Region

One troubling feature of the method presented so far is the vast amount of space in the underflow region between zero and the smallest magnitude number. It is more preferable to have an evenly distributed set of values capable of filling this region to induce a so-called 'gradual underflow'. In order to do this, some of the 'scrunched up' numbers near the boundary of the normalized region will be reassigned to the underflow region.

Gradual Underflow
We will make further use of the case where the binary representation of the exponent is a string of zeros.

If the **Exponent = -n (excess n)** and
- a) **Significand = 0** → represent $(0)_{10}$ (as already discussed above)
- b) **Significand ≠ 0** → assume
  - i. Hidden bit = 0 (i.e. instead of hidden bit = 1, use '**denormalized**' numbers)
  - ii. Exponent string of zeros redefined to be $(-n+1)_{10}$

Example
Consider converting the following sequence to decimal

| 0 | 000 | 1001 |

i.   First, since the exponent is a string of zeros and the significand is not a string of zeros, the converted number will be **denormalized** (i.e. *the hidden bit is assumed to be zero*).

ii.   Second, the exponent will not be interpreted using excess 3, but, instead will be taken to be **offset** (-3+1) =-2.

Hence, according to the above definition for gradual underflow

$$\text{Hidden Bit} = 0$$
$$\text{Exponent} = -2 \text{ (not -3)}$$

and, the equivalent fractional binary number becomes

$$0\ 000\ 1001 = +0.1001 \times 2^{-2}$$
$$= (+0.001001)_2$$
$$= (+0.140625)_{10}$$

Let's put the revised representation in context by listing numbers up to the boundary of the normalized region. In this table, FP refers to the 'floating point' representation.

	FP	$= (\ )_2$	$= (\ )_{10}$
Normalized Positive Boundary	0 001 0000	$+1.0000 \times 2^{-2}$	+0.25
	0 000 1111	$+0.1111 \times 2^{-2}$	+0.234375
	.	.	.
	.	.	.
	0 000 0001	$+0.0001 \times 2^{-2}$	+0.015625
Denormalized Region	0 000 0000	+0.0	+0.0
	1 000 0000	-0.0	-0.0
	1 000 0001	-0.0001×2^{-2}	-0.015625
	.	.	.
	.	.	.
	1 000 1111	-0.1111×2^{-2}	-0.234375
Normalized Negative Boundary	1 001 0000	-1.0000×2^{-2}	-0.25

Important Observations

- The smallest magnitude number is the smallest increment: 0.015625 (as opposed to $1.0001 \times 2^{-3} = 0.1328125$)
- Numbers in the denormalized region are equally separated.
- The benefit of the excess representation for the exponent begins to become apparent. Notice how the first seven bits (excluding the sign bit) are naturally arranged in unsigned order for both positive and negative numbers; thereby, potentially simplifying the comparison of numerical magnitudes. More on this in a moment.
- Given that the 000 exponent bit pattern was sacrificed to enable representation of the denormalized region, changing the offset from -3 (excess 3) to an offset of -2 allows for a sensible numerical transition to the normalized region.

Inf and NaN

Let us conclude our journey by addressing cases where overflow or illogical calculations might occur. Again, some bits in the representation will have to be sacrificed in order to accommodate such cases. Let us begin with some definitions.

Inf = 'Infinity' assigned to values in the overflow region

Inf obeys the basic algebraic rules one might expect from infinity

$$x + \infty = +\infty$$
$$x - \infty = -\infty$$
$$\infty + \infty = +\infty$$

and so on.

NaN = 'Not a Number' assigned to values that are not allowed

NaN tries to take in account all other possible cases where a given answer does not exist or the resulting data type is not supported. For example, under certain conditions, a calculation such as 0/0 could result in NaN as the output. In addition, invoking informal algebraic rules such as

$$x + NaN = NaN$$
$$x/NaN = NaN$$

allow for the possibility, if desired, of uninterrupted program flow when such situations are encountered.

Representing Inf and NaN

In order to represent Inf and NaN, the following choice is made:

Reserve the <u>largest possible exponent</u> (i.e. a string of all ones) for Inf and Nan.
  i. Significand = 0 → Inf
 ii. Significand ≠ 0 → NaN

Clearly, since the bits for the largest exponent have been sacrificed to represent these cases, the range between the maximum and minimum values will be reduced. Again, considering our 8-bit example, we can illustrate how this choice affects the range.

	FP	= ( )$_{10}$
	0 111 xxxx	NaN
	0 111 0000	+Inf
Normalized Positive Upper Boundary	0 110 1111 . . .	+15.5 . . .
	0 000 0000	+0.0
	1 000 0000	-0.0
Normalized Negative Lower Boundary	. . . 1 110 1111	. . . -15.5
	1 111 0000	-Inf
	1 111 xxxx	NaN

where 'xxxx' refers to any 4-bit binary sequence that is not a string of zeros. Given this choice, notice how the relative magnitude is still preserved by the first seven bits when the sign bit is excluded.

Representation Summary

The finer details of the floating point representation for our 8-bit example are summarized in the following table:

	FP	$= ( )_2$	$= ( )_{10}$
NaN	0 111 xxxx		
+Inf	0 111 0000		
Positive Normalized	0 110 1111 . . 0 001 0000	$+1.1111 \times 2^4$ . . $+1.0000 \times 2^{-2}$	+15.5 . . +0.25
Positive Denormalized	0 000 1111 . . 0 000 0001	$+0.1111 \times 2^{-2}$ . . $+0.0001 \times 2^{-2}$	+0.234375 . . +0.015625
Zero	0 000 0000 1 000 0000	+0.0 -0.0	+0.0 -0.0
Negative Denormalized	1 000 0001 . . 1 000 1111	-0.0001×2^{-2} . . -0.1111×2^{-2}	-0.015625 . . -0.234375
Negative Normalized	1 001 0000 . . 1 110 1111	-1.0000×2^{-2} . . -1.1111×2^4	-0.25 . . -15.5
-Inf	1 111 0000		
NaN	1 111 xxxx		

Exercise

Fill in some more values in the summary table for the 8-bit representation to make sure you understand normalized versus denormalized numbers.

i. (*Justifying the use of the Excess n representation for the exponent*). Pay close attention to the first seven bits and observe how the ordering of those unsigned binary sequences respect the relative magnitudes of each represented number.

ii. Pay close attention to the smallest increment achievable given the bit precision of the significand.

Chapter Eight: The IEEE 754 Standard for Representing Floating Point Numbers

We have come quite a distance in traversing from binary fractional numbers to the floating point representation introduced in the previous chapter. In this chapter we introduce the IEEE 754 standard used in most computer systems for representing floating point numbers. To do this, the 8-bit example previously discussed will have to be extended to more bits. While the IEEE 754 standard applies the same structure already introduced,

[Sign | Exponent | Significand]

details regarding the number of bits will define the precision (and, therefore, the variable type).

Definitions

a. **Single Precision** = 32 bits (4 bytes)
   - Example: 'float' in C++

   Sign bit = 1 bit
   Exponent = 8 bits
         Normalized numbers➔ excess 127
         Denormalized ➔ exponent = -126
   Significand = 23 bits

Sign (1 bit)	Exponent (8 bits)	Significand (23 bits)

b. **Double Precision** = 64 bits (8 bytes)
- Example: 'float64' in Python

   Sign bit = 1 bit
   Exponent = 11 bits
      Normalized numbers➜ excess 1023
      Denormalized ➜ exponent = -1022
   Significand = 52 bits

Sign (1 bit)	Exponent (11 bits)	Significand (52 bits)

c. **Quadruple Precision ('binary128')** =128 bits (16 bytes)

   Sign bit = 1 bit
   Exponent = 15 bits
      Normalized numbers➜ excess 16383
      Denormalized ➜ exponent = -16382
   Significand = 112 bits

Sign (1 bit)	Exponent (15 bits)	Significand (112 bits)

d. **Octuple Precision ('binary256')** = 256 bits (32 bytes)

   Sign bit = 1 bit
   Exponent = 19 bits
      Normalized numbers➜ excess (2^{18}-1)
      Denormalized ➜ exponent = -(2^{18}-2)
   Significand = 236 bits

Sign (1 bit)	Exponent (19 bits)	Significand (236 bits)

Let's include hexadecimal values as shorthand for the lengthy binary sequences and analyze some examples.

+Inf (single precision)
+Inf = 0 | 1111 1111 | 000 0000 0000 0000 0000 0000
     = 0111 1111 1000 0000 0000 0000 0000 0000
     = $(7F80\ 0000)_{16}$

Smallest Normalized Number (single precision)
     0| 0000 0001 | 000 0000 0000 0000 0000 0000
         = $(+1.0 \times 2^{-126})$

Converting the associated binary sequence to hexadecimal yields
     = 0000 0000 1000 0000 0000 0000 0000 0000
     = $(0080\ 0000)_{16}$

Smallest Denormalized Number (single precision)
     0| 0000 0000 | 000 0000 0000 0000 0000 0001
         = $(0.00000000000000000000001 \times 2^{-126})$
         = $2^{-149} \approx 1.4 \times 10^{-45}$
and this number also represents the smallest magnitude single precision increment. Converting the associated binary sequence to hexadecimal yields
     = 0000 0000 0000 0000 0000 0000 0000 0001
     = $(0000\ 0001)_{16}$

Smallest Denormalized Number (double precision)
     $(0000\ 0000\ 0000\ 0001)_{16}$
         = $(0.0000\ ....\ 0001 \times 2^{-1022})$
         = $2^{-1074} \approx 1.0 \times 10^{-323}$
and this number also represents the smallest magnitude double precision increment.

Examples

The following examples will hopefully pull together the concepts introduced in this text so far.

a. Convert $(-103.75)_{10}$ to IEEE 754 Single Precision

Convert the numerical part to fractional binary and then to normalized scientific notation

$103 = 0110\ 0111$
$0.75 = 0.110$
→ $103.75 = (01100111.110)_2$
$= 1.100111110 \times 2^6$

Now convert the exponent to excess 127

$6+127 = (133)_{10} = 1000\ 0101$ (excess 127)

Since the number is negative, the sign bit = 1. Combing the significand, the exponent and the sign bit leads to the single precision result

$1\ |\ 1000\ 0101\ |\ 1001\ 1111\ 0000\ 0000\ 0000\ 000$
$= 1100\ 0010\ 1100\ 1111\ 1000\ 0000\ 0000\ 0000$
$= (C2CF\ 8000)_{16}$

b. Convert $(41A3\ 0000)_{16}$ IEEE 754 Single Precision

$(41A3\ 0000)_{16}$
$= 0100\ 0001\ 1010\ 0011\ 0000\ 0000\ 0000\ 0000$
$= 0\ |\ 1000\ 0011\ |\ 0100\ 0110\ 0000\ 0000\ 0000\ 000$

Sign Bit = 0 (positive)
Exponent = $1000\ 0011$ excess 127
Convert to decimal
→ $131 - 127 = +4$
Normalized Significand = 1.01000110
→ $1.01000110 \times 2^4 = (10100.0110)_2$
$= (+20.375)_{10}$

c. Convert (803D 0000)$_{16}$ IEEE 754 Single Precision

(803D 0000)$_{16}$
= 1000 0000 0011 1101 0000 0000 0000 0000
= 1 | 0000 0000 | 0111 1010 0000 0000 0000 000

Sign bit = 1 (negative)
Exponent = 0000 0000
    → denormalized number with exponent = -126
    since significand is nonzero.
Denormalized Significand = 0.01111010
→ -0.01111010 x 2^{-126} = -1.11101 x 2^{-128}
                ≈ -5.601965265637464 x 10^{-39}

Chapter Nine: Program Verification of the Floating Point Representation

This is an *optional chapter topic* that can be skipped if the reader has minimal programming experience. Given the IEEE 754 standard, we propose an exercise that will enable one to inspect and verify the IEEE 754 bit structure of a floating point variable declared within a computer program. The process requires referencing the memory location of a given stored floating point number. This could, for example, be accomplished with an assembly language. However, any high level language that makes provision for pointers will also suffice. In this chapter we choose to apply C++.

Please note that the proposed method is not the same as performing the decimal to binary conversion of a floating point number. Algorithms to do this have already been discussed. The process suggested here only requires determining the bit pattern associated with some integer value; however, the bits generated will be the sign bit, the exponent and the significand associated with the floating point variable expressed in IEEE 754 format.

In C++, the 'float' data type is single precision and the 'int' data type is 4-byte signed 2's complement. Since both data types are 32 bits in length, this leads us to the following approach:
   a. Recast a given floating point value in single precision IEEE 754 format as an integer,
   b. Output the bits of the integer.

Consider a sample C++ code snippet that will implement these steps for the 4-byte case:
```
//=====================
        //Declare variables
        float a=-103.75;
        int m=32;       //4 bytes=32 bits
        int n;          //'n' will hold resulting integer
        int j;
```

```
//The variable 'a' must be viewed
//as a 4–byte integer. This is achieved
//by recasting the address
//of 'a' as a pointer to an integer.
n= *(int *) &a;

//This loop will output the bits of 'n' using a
//loop of left shifts that inspect
//the MSB (i.e. the sign bit) of 'n'
for (j=0; j<m; j++)
        {
        if (n<0)
                cout << "1" << endl;
        else
                cout << "0" << endl;
         n=2*n;
        }
```

Exercise

After compiling this code snippet and ensuring its correctness, go back to the previous chapter and verify the examples demonstrating the IEEE 754 format for single precision.

Chapter Ten: Floating Point Arithmetic

Now that we have a grasp of the floating point representation, let's apply this knowledge to performing arithmetic operations. The intent of this chapter is to serve as a basic introduction; hence, we merely 'skim the surface' of the fundamental rudiments of addition and multiplication. Since the floating point representation is naturally related to scientific notation, the goal for this chapter is simply to review and highlight the algorithmic logic behind the processing of the sign bit, the exponent and the significand. As there are a spectrum of details involved in the potential mixing of normalized numbers with denormalized numbers, zero, Inf and NaN, to maintain the discussion at an introductory level, we will exclude discussions regarding those cases.

Notation

Given two floating point operands A and B, we will refer to the sign bits, the exponents and the significands using the following notation:

B_A = sign bit of A $\qquad$ B_B = sign bit of B
E_A = exponent of A $\qquad$ E_B = exponent of B
S_A = significand of A $\qquad$ S_B = significand of B

Addition

The addition of numbers presented in scientific notation requires the exponents of the operands to be the same so that the significands can be added. Under these circumstances, it is sensible to determine the lesser of the two operand exponents and convert the numerical form to that of the greater exponent.

Compute A+B as follows:
> **Step 1**: If $E_A \neq E_B$, determine the operand with the lesser of the two exponents.
> **Step 2**: Convert the lesser exponent to the greater exponent by adding the absolute value of the difference
> $$D_{AB} = |E_A - E_B|$$
> to the lesser exponent.
> **Step 3**: Right shift the associated significand by D_{AB} places.
> **Step 4**: Perform the binary addition of the significands assuming they are aligned at the decimal point.
> **Step 5**: Perform 'post-normalization' of the result to convert it to normalized form (as outlined in Chapter 4).

Multiplication

Multiplication of numbers in scientific notation requires adding the exponents of the operands and multiplying the significands. To do this, we must be aware that exponents are represented using excess n.

Compute A+B as follows:
> **Step 1**: Perform multiplication of the significands.
> **Step 2**: Add the exponents assuming excess n.
> **Step 3**: Sign bit of the result = $XOR(B_A, B_B)$ (i.e. the exclusive OR).
> **Step 4**: Perform 'post-normalization' of the result to put in normalized form.

The outline provided above reveals the basic steps necessary for arithmetic assuming the floating point representation. A deeper discussion would involve greater details for performing the various binary additions and multiplications (for example, as introduced in Volume 1) as well as encompassing the necessary host of special cases.

Made in the USA
Las Vegas, NV
20 November 2023

81201428R00038